The Joy of Holiday Music

**Celebrating throughout the year with best-loved songs and effective piano solos.
A collection by Denes Agay.**

Order No. YK 21850
US International Standard Book Number: 0.8256.8104.9
UK International Standard Book Number: 0.7119.6776.8

Exclusive Distributors:
Music Sales Corporation
257 Park Avenue South, New York, NY 10010 USA
Music Sales Limited
8/9 Frith Street, London W1D 3JB England
Music Sales Pty. Limited
120 Rothschild Street, Rosebery, Sydney, NSW 2018, Australia

Printed in the United States of America by
Vicks Lithograph and Printing Corporation

Yorktown Music Press, Inc.
New York/London/Paris/Sydney/Copenhagen/Madrid

Contents

Auld Lang Syne

Scottish Air

Hail! Hail! The Gang's All Here

Arthur Sullivan

A New Year Waltz
Auld Lang Syne

Denes Agay

Ring Out, Wild Bells

Alfred Tennyson

Wolfgang Amadeus Mozart

2. Ring out the old, ring in the new,
Ring, happy bells, across the snow:
The year is going, let him go;
Ring out the false, ring in the true.

3. Ring out false pride in place and blood,
The civic slander and the spite;
Ring in the love of truth and right,
Ring in the common love of good.

We Shall Overcome

Spiritual

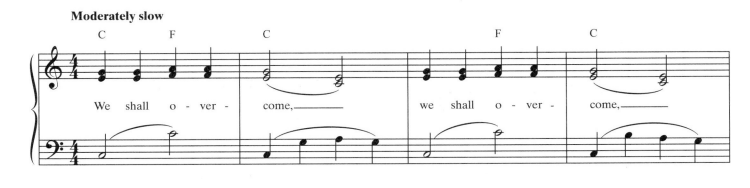

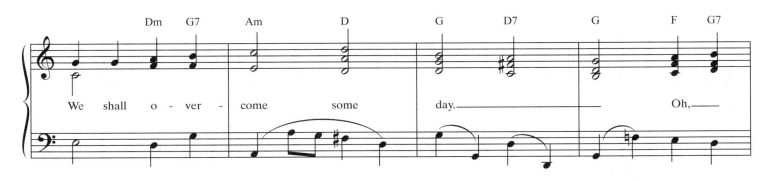

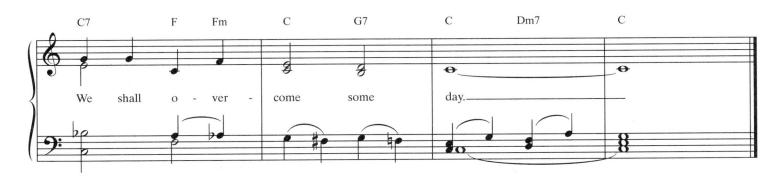

2. We shall walk in peace,
   We shall walk in peace,
   We shall walk in peace some day.
   Oh, deep in my heart
   I do believe
   We shall walk in peace some day.

3. We shall build a new world,
   We shall build a new world,
   We shall build a new world some day.
   Oh, deep in my heart
   I do believe
   We shall build a new world some day.

Oh, Freedom

Spiritual

I Love You Truly

Carrie Jacobs Bond

Let Me Call You Sweetheart

Beth Slater Whitson

Leo Friedman

Lyrics:

Let me call you sweet-heart, I'm in love with you. Let me hear you whis-per that you love me too. Keep the love - light glow-ing in your eyes so true, Let me call you sweet-heart, I'm in love with you.

For Mary
A Golden Valentine

Denes Agay

I Love You

Edvard Grieg

Salut d'Amour

Love's Greeting

Sir Edward Elgar

Hail to the Chief

Sir Walter Scott

James Sanderson

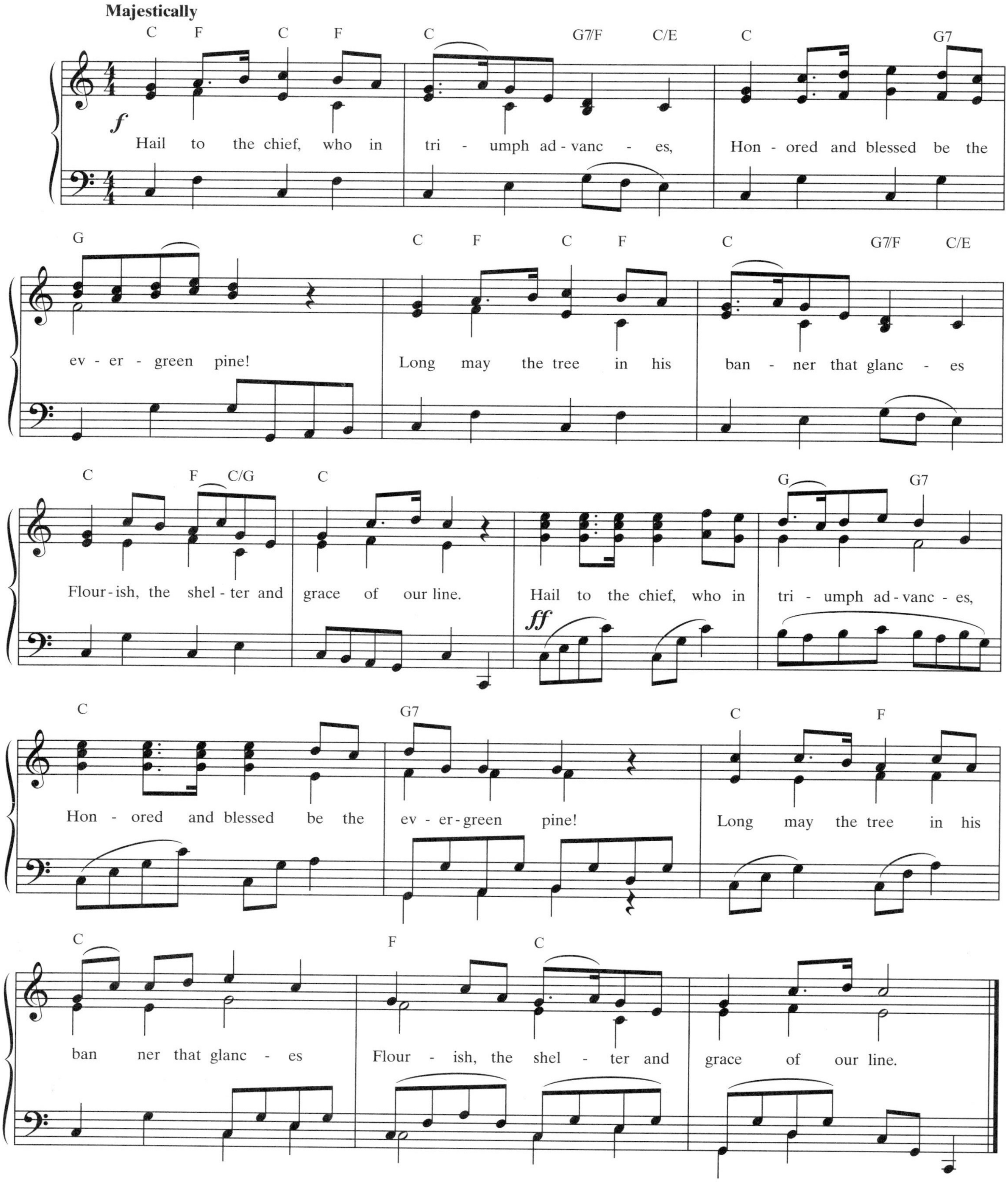

Irish Rhapsody

Adapted by Denes Agay

Lively *The Irish Washerwoman*

When Irish Eyes Are Smiling

Chauncey Olcott
George Graff, Jr.

Ernest R. Ball
James Royce Shannon

Too-Ra-Loo-Ra-Loo-Ral

(That's an Irish Lullaby)

James Royce Shannon

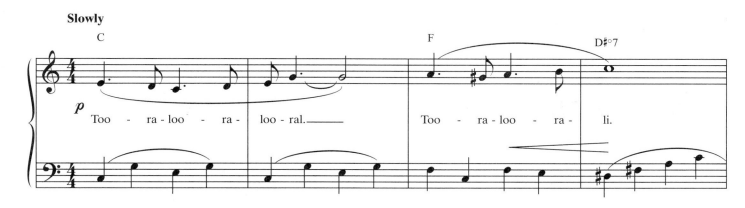

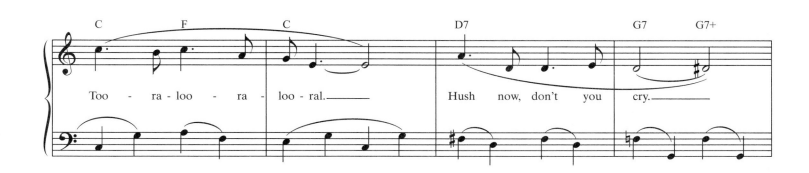

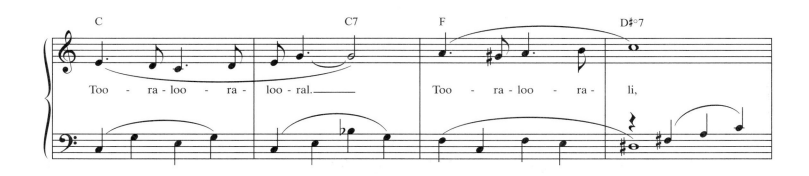

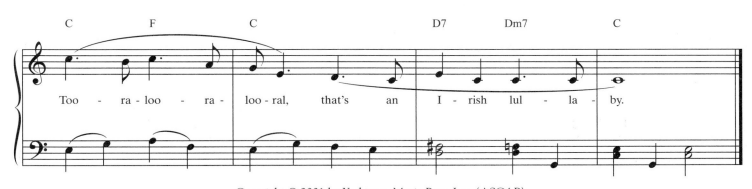

Praise the Lord

Passover chant

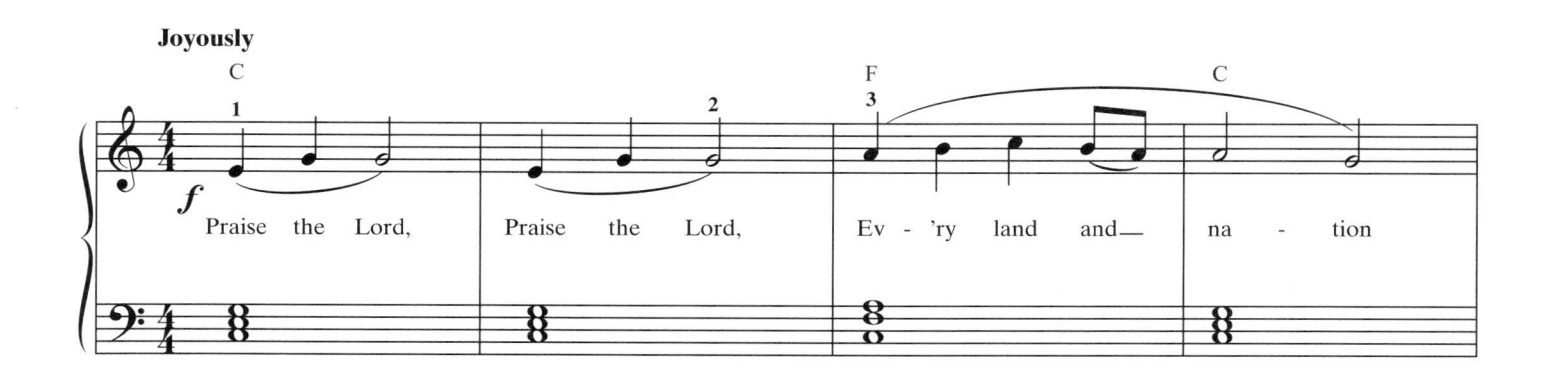

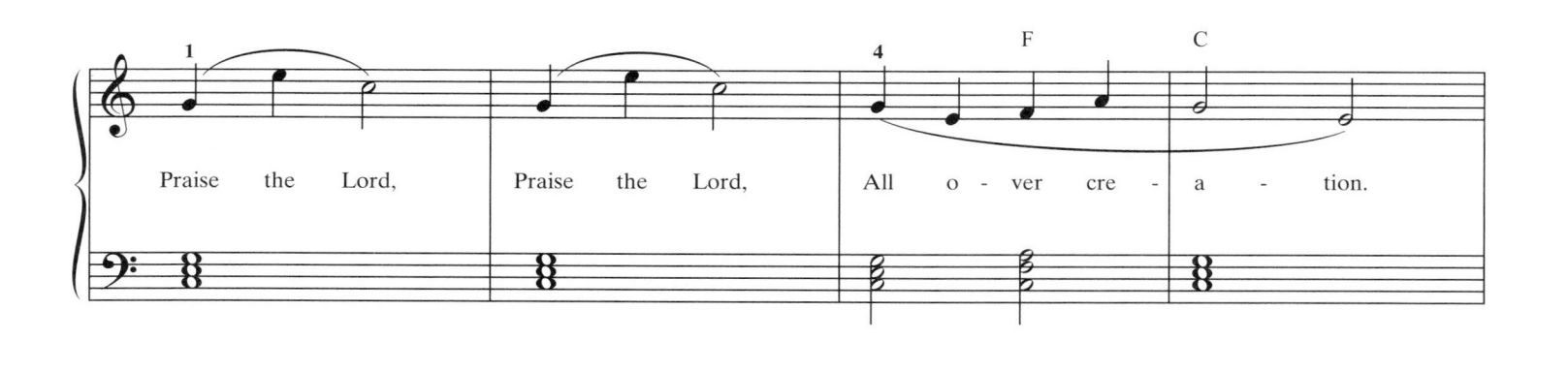

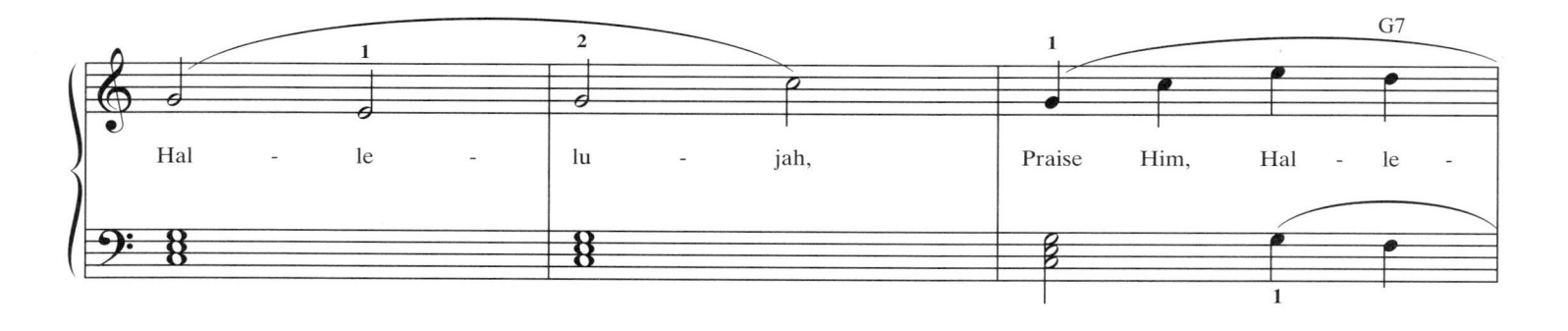

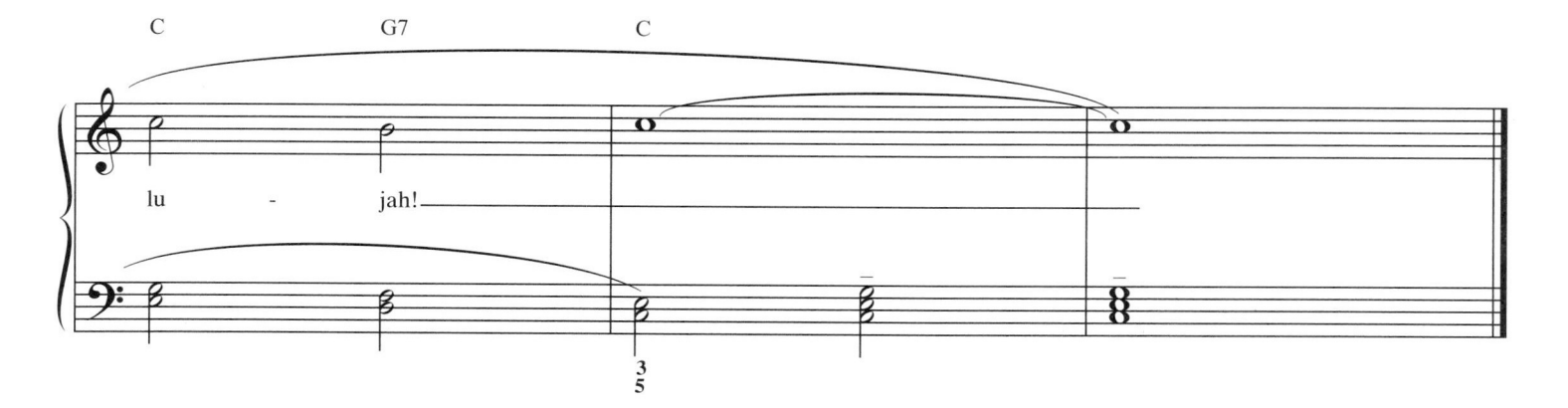

Were You There?

Spiritual

2. Were you there, when they nailed him to the tree?
Were you there, when they nailed him to the tree?
Oh— sometimes, it causes me to tremble,
    tremble, tremble,
Were you there, when they nailed him to the tree?

3. Were you there, when the sun refused to shine?
Were you there, when the sun refused to shine?
Oh— sometimes, it causes me to tremble,
    tremble, tremble,
Were you there, when the sun refused to shine?

I Know that My Redeemer Liveth

from "Messiah"

George Frideric Handel

The Palms

Jean-Baptiste Faure

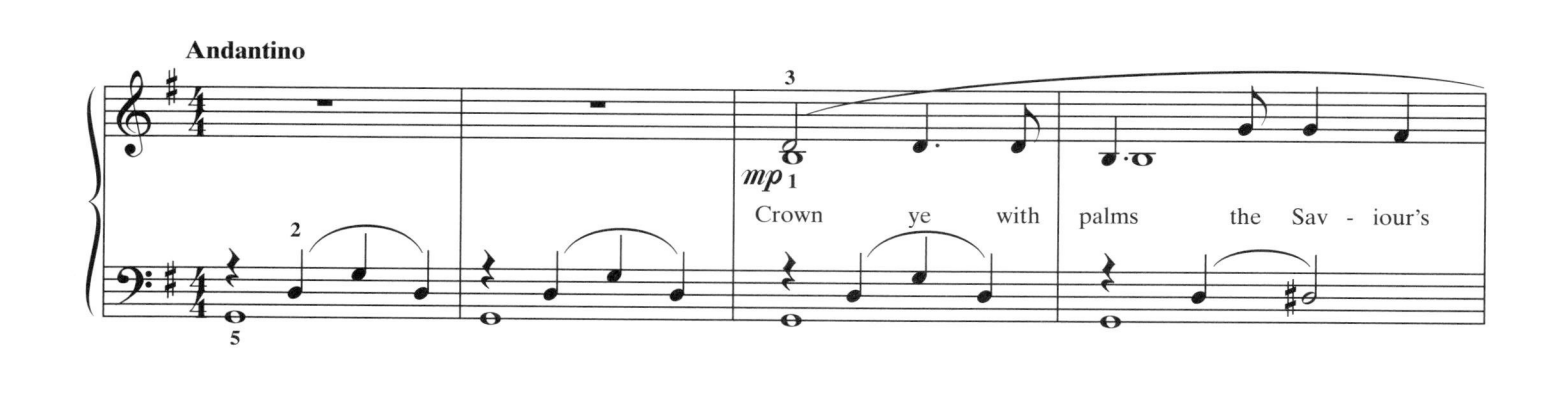

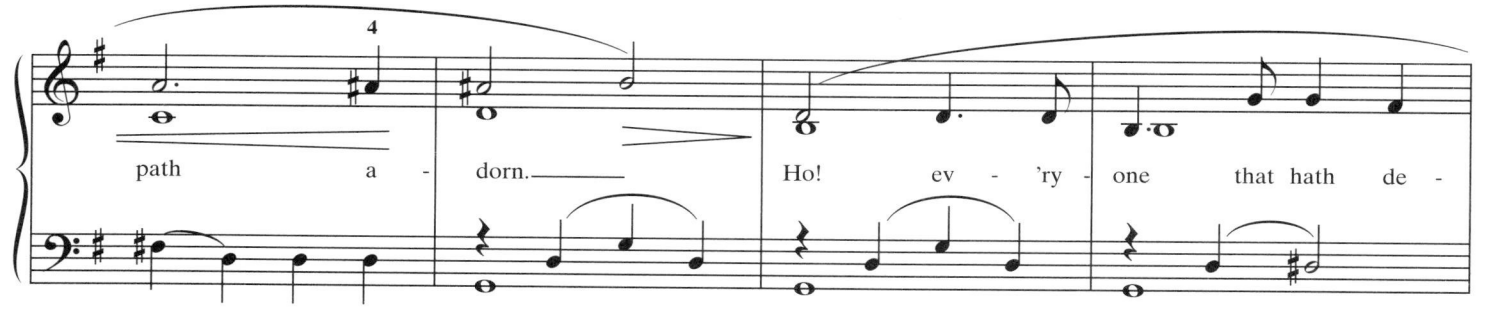

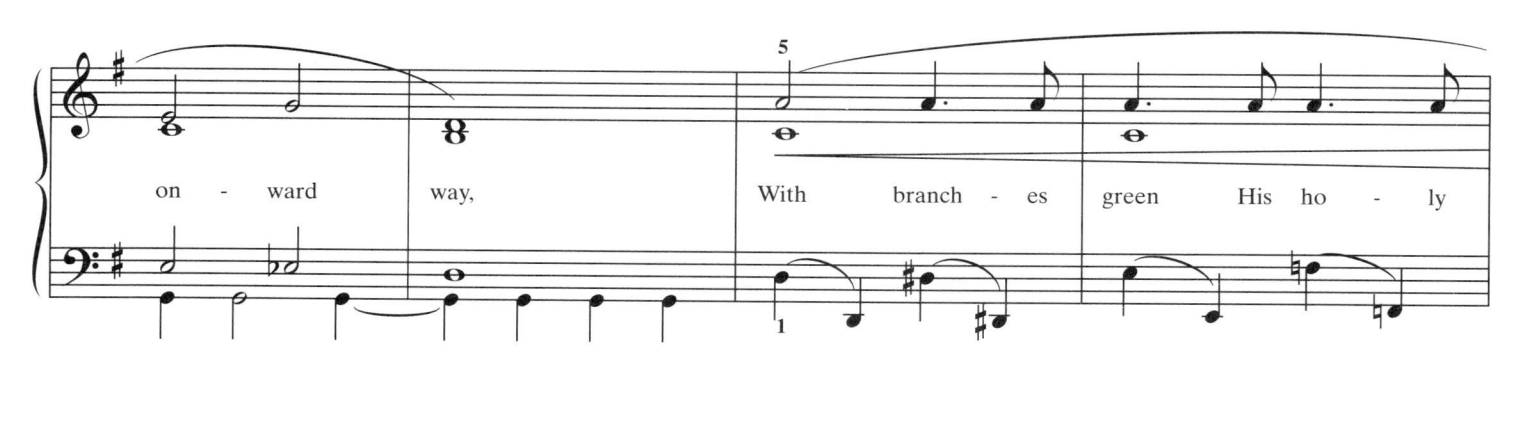

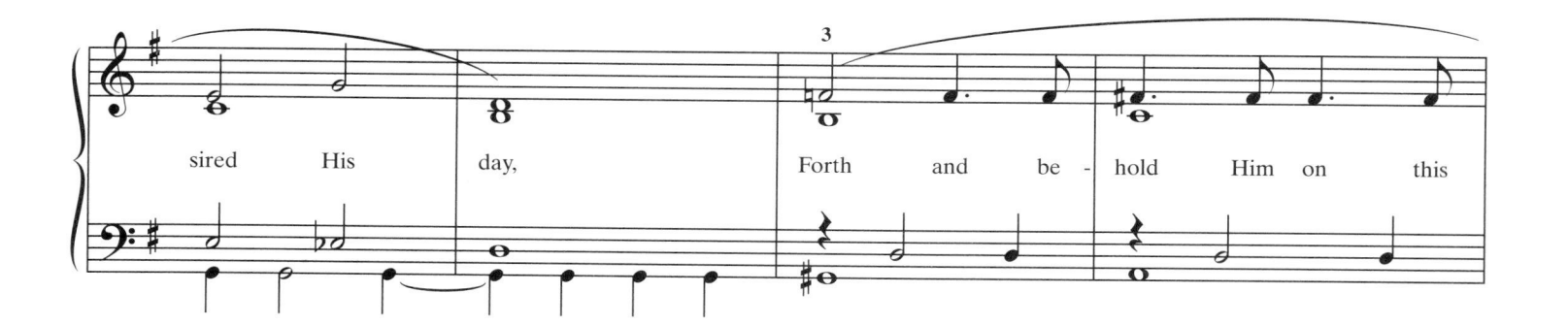

fes - tal morn! Ju - dah re - joice! with one ac - cord, From earth to heav - en let our voi - ces wave, Ho - san - na! Hail to the Lord! Ho - ly is He, who comes the world to save!

Allargando

Hallelujah
from "Messiah"

George Frideric Handel
Arranged by Frank Metis

Album Leaf for Mother

(Song My Mother Taught Me)

Antonín Dvořák

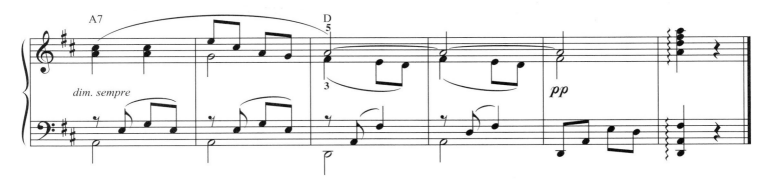

Amazing Grace

Rev. John Newton

Folk hymn

2. 'Twas grace that taught my heart to fear,
And grace my fears relieved;
How precious did that grace appear
The hour I first believed.

3. Thro' many dangers toils and snares,
I have already come;
'Tis grace that bro't me safe thus far,
And grace will lead me home.

4. How sweet the name of Jesus sounds
In a believer's ear;
It sooths his sorrows, heals his wounds,
And drives away his fear.

5. Must Jesus bear the cross alone
And all the world go free?
No, there's a cross for ev'ry one
And there's a cross for me.

M-O-T-H-E-R

(A Word That Means the World to Me)

Howard Johnson

Theodore F. Morse

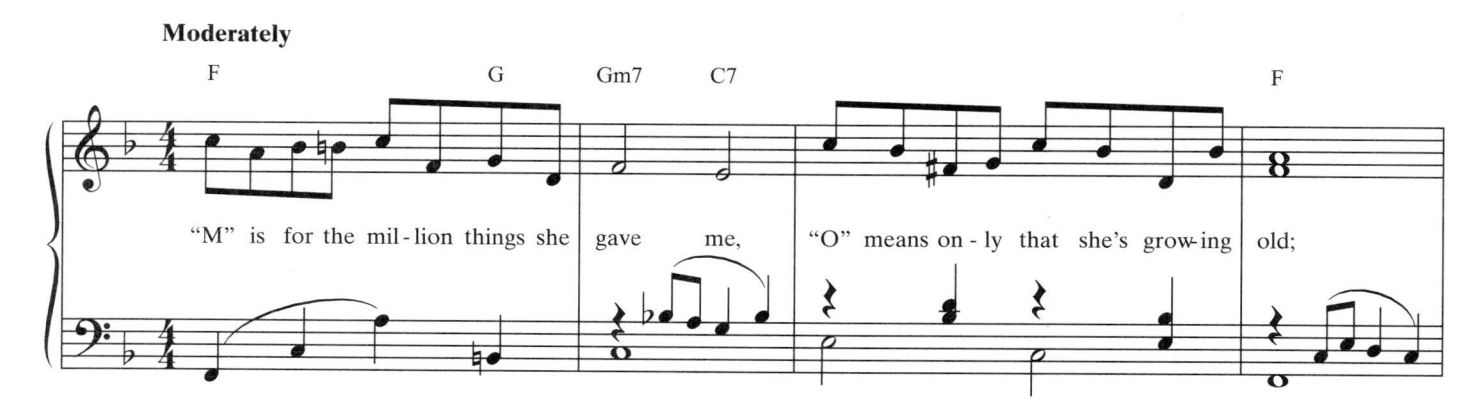

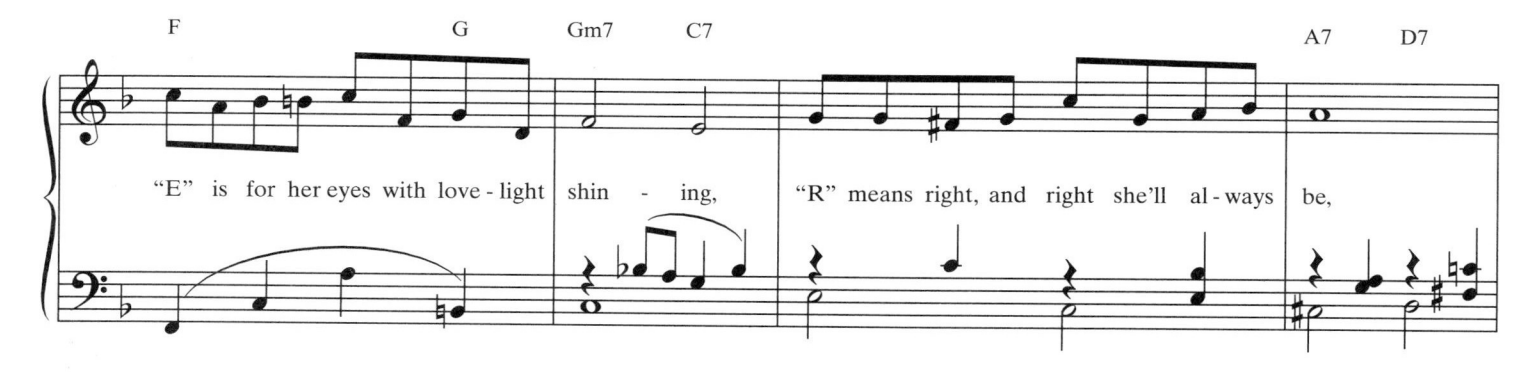

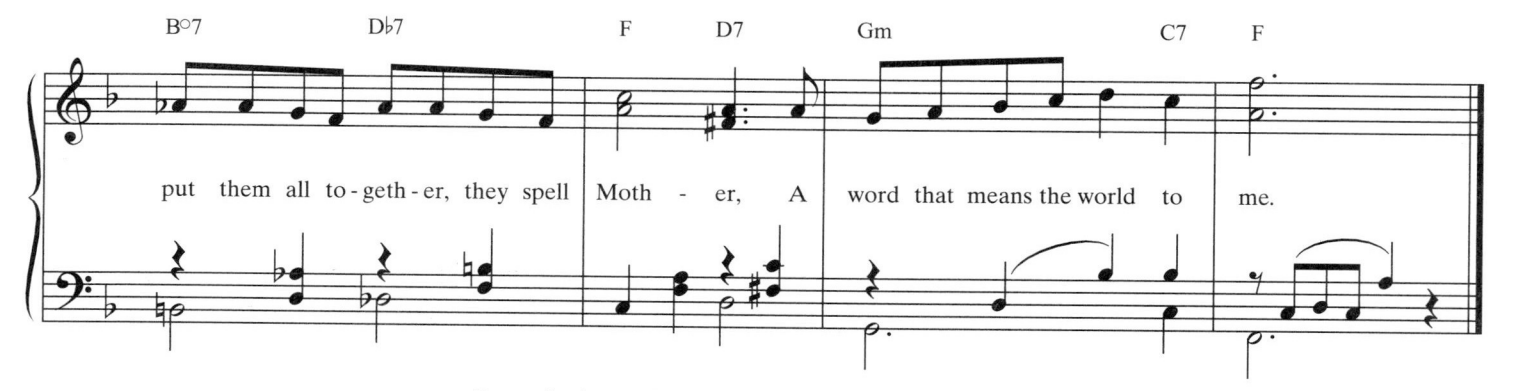

Battle Hymn of the Republic

Julia Ward Howe

Traditional

The Stars and Stripes Forever

John Philip Sousa

39

You're a Grand Old Flag

George M. Cohan

For He's a Jolly Good Fellow

(*a modern version*)

Traditional
Adapted by Frank Metis

Fanfare for Father's Day
(For He's a Jolly Good Fellow)

Denes Agay

Yankee Doodle

with Variations

Anonymous
(c.1790)

The Star-Spangled Banner

Francis Scott Key

John Stafford Smith

Prelude on "The Star-Spangled Banner"

Denes Agay

Boogie Macabre*

Denes Agay

The Marionette's Funeral March

Charles Gounod

Walking tempo; with mock mystery

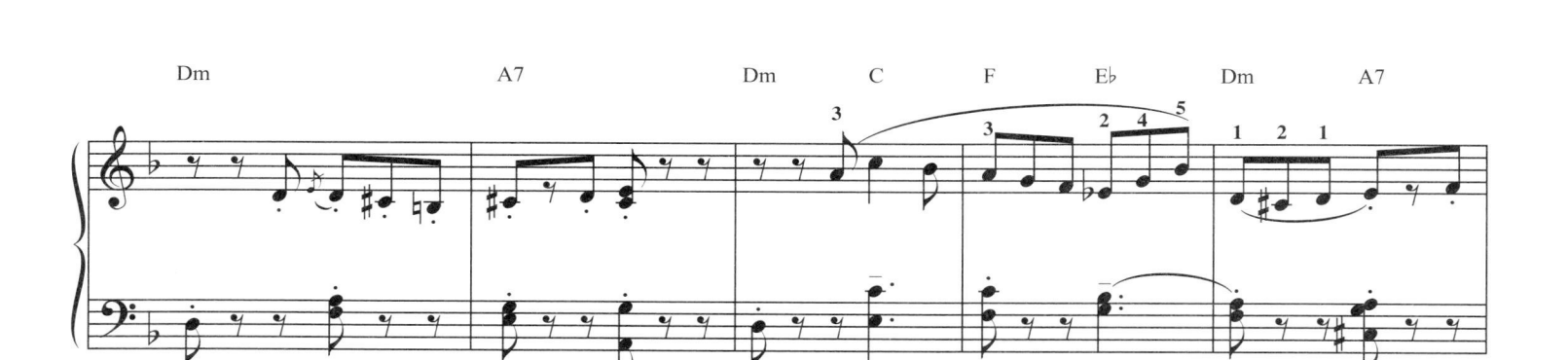

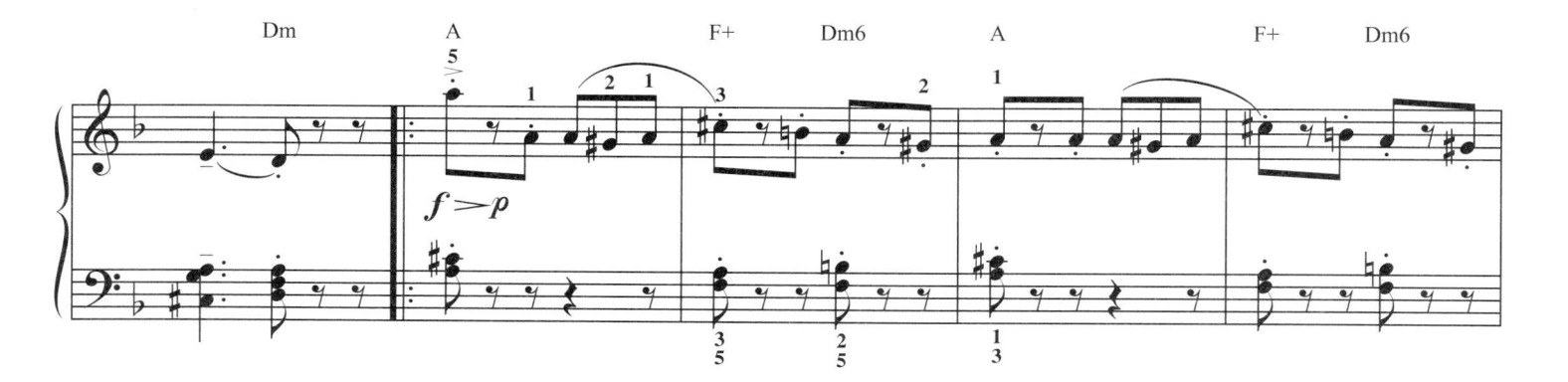

Armed Forces Medley

Arranged by Frank Metis

The Marine's Hymn

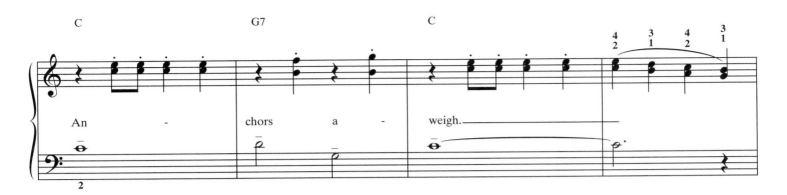

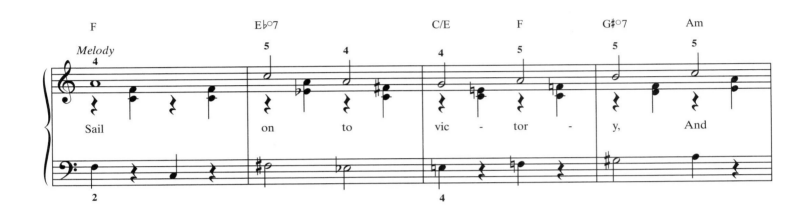

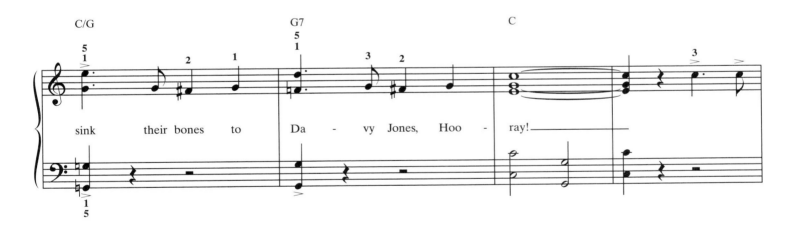

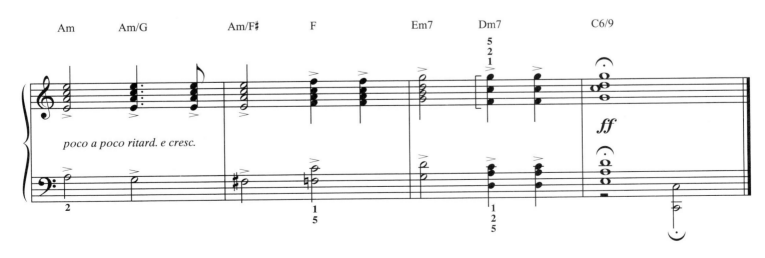

Over the River and through the Woods

O-ver the riv-er and through the woods, To grand-fa-ther's house we go;————— The horse knows the way to car-ry the sleigh, Thro' the white and drift-ed snow.———— O-ver the riv-er and thro' the woods, Oh how the wind does blow!———— It stings the toes And bites the nose, As o-ver the ground we go.————

Prayer of Thanksgiving

Wilt Heden Nu Treden

Dutch hymn

Now Thank We All Our God

Martin Rinckart

Johann Crüger

A Chanukah Song

(Ma'oz Tzur)

Traditional

The Dreydl Song

Play Tune at Chanukah

Traditional

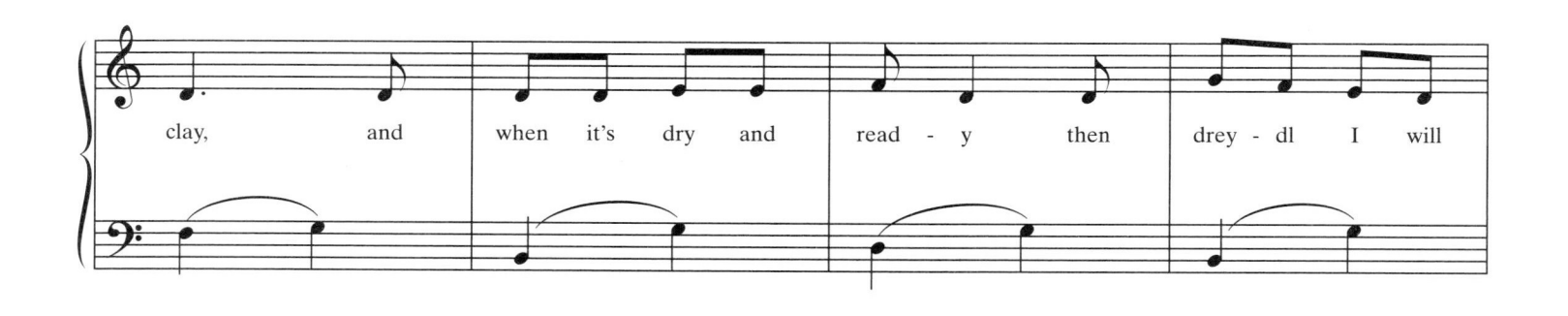

We Wish You a Merry Christmas

English carol

2. Oh, bring us some figgy pudding,
   Oh, bring us some figgy pudding,
   Oh, bring us some figgy pudding,
   And bring it out here! *Chorus:*

3. We won't go until we got some,
   We won't go until we got some,
   We won't go until we got some,
   So bring some out here. *Chorus:*

Christmas Prelude

(Oh Come, All Ye Faithful)

Denes Agay

Deck the Hall

Welsh carol

Silent Night

Franz X. Gruber

O Holy Night

Cantique De Noël

Adolphe Adam

Jingle Bells Jazz

James S. Pierpont
Adapted by Frank Metis

"Happy Birthday" with Variations

Adapted by Denes Agay

Allegretto cantabile (... à la Mozart)